SPEAKING
—TO—
YOUR SOUL

SPEAKING
—TO—
YOUR SOUL
Poetry for the mind, body and soul.

SOUL SISTAH

ARPress
ILLUMINATING IDEAS
EMPOWERING VOICES

ARPress
45 Dan Road Suite 5
Canton MA 02021

Hotline: 1(800) 220-7660
Fax: 1(855) 752-6001

Ordering Information:
Quantity sales. Special discounts are available on quantity purchases by corporations, associations, and others. For details, contact the publisher at the address above.

Printed in the United States of America.

ISBN-13:   Paperback   979-8-89389-020-4
            eBook   979-8-89389-021-1

Library of Congress Control Number: 2024908168

Contents

Inspirational Poetry

"Living Testament"

The cracks in the foundation
of my life took years to repair.

It was left with no
acknowledgment or care.

Every day was a struggle, as
I fought with myself while juggling
and living a double life of pretending
to be happy when all I wanted to do was scream.

It's crazy how those on the outside get
a small view and think you're doing good
but in reality, things aren't always
what they seem.

Walking when I wanted to fly,
laughing when I really wanted to cry.
Giving up and losing the will to try breaks
your self-esteem and tarnishes your dreams.

I am a living testament that despite my
mental breakdown, I found my escape to
free myself from myself.

The self that wasn't capable of healing,
loving, or giving.

But, through my ancestors' willingness, I was
saved and the chance to live again with no pain,
I was given.

I am now staring at the foundation that was
once filled with cracks slowly
but surely getting its confidence
back despite the scars left behind.

The scars I'm leaving behind!

Conflicted, is this love or a sickness?
Am I infatuated or using
you to escape the reality of
my conscious that taunts me and haunts
my inner peace.

Do I see you as my sanctuary
or have we buried the last existence of
our emotions by keeping them tucked
away in the deep dark spaces of our mind?

Sometimes, I find myself lingering
on the hopes that we would reconnect
and reject those feelings that create doubt.
We'd avoid the possibility of
wanting to walk out and stand strong
on this bond we built.

But, is this a real bond or a trauma that bonded
us from our past fears and experiences?

I've become so disillusioned that
I'm constantly jumping to conclusions
over the anxiety of losing you,
but the real question is who is losing who?

The agony and pain is really
driving me insane, I no longer consider
this love, more so a game.

There are levels to this,
but we've run out of ammunition to
savor the last moments of our connection
which is now disconnected.
The hurt is filling the places in our hearts
we once had reserved for one another.

I can't see us not being with each other,
but I feel as though
I'm being smothered by my fear
of being alone.

At the same time I can continue
with this charade of thinking what
we have is real, so I'm
writing this letter to tell you how I feel.

As time goes on those unanswered
questions that were never answered will be
revealed, I just pray we don't view
what we had as a tragedy or
a moment short-lived.

I love you,
I need you yet my heart,
body and mind are no
longer full from your love.
I don't have the energy to
give you or time to feed you
with my beautiful words and
reassuring thoughts.

So, I'm leaving maybe one day
we will meet again and
figure out that we were always
connected even when we were miles apart.
Goodbye anxiety, depression,
and fears of rejection.

I am reclaiming my life and living again!

Changes

I see no changes, wake up in the morning
and I ask myself, how much of living
my life is left?

Another hashtag added to the growing numbers
of police brutality, modern-day lynching is
no longer a thing of the past,
It's a new reality that keeps happening.

All we can feel is anger, and sadness,
as we relive old racism in an already corrupt nation.
Shopping, walking and running added
to the list of things you can't do while Black.

How do I continue surviving
when there's a target on my back?
I cry for the mothers, sisters,
and brothers who have to mourn the
loss of a loved one murdered by the police.

We must take a stand, how many more have to die
from the hands of the slave patrol?
Will we keep crying and marching
or finally, rise up and control our right to live?

Will, we be guilted and choose to forgive
our enemies?

Who shows us every day that no matter
how many tears
we shed no changes or sympathy
will be sent our way.

As we live through this old age racism
our grandmothers and grandfathers
fought through every day.

They did it all without letting
defeat be their end.

If we don't stand for something
we'll lose the battle and
the war will never end.

Rip to George Floyd and the many
others who were viciously
murdered in modern-day lynching
also known as police brutality.

I just want to be free!

Trapped in a world filled with stereotypes and
false statistics, being labeled an animal because you
had enough, so for a moment, you go ballistic.

Standing in a room with people who don't see you as
their equal leaves me angry and on edge.
Negative thoughts
constantly crowd my head,
why does society hate the Black race?

As I lay here deep in thought about
restoring my faith in humanity,
I often daydream and wonder what
God has planned for me, there are
people who want to see me down,
but I refuse to be, so I stand for me.

I just want to be free,
I just need to release myself from the world
so filled with hate.

So, many misunderstood souls cry out to be saved,
the young generation's minds are being controlled
by the media turning them into slaves.

Education is a gift, but it's the streets they crave,
living a life that has consequences;
some end up in jail or a grave.

As I continue expressing these thoughts, I feel as
though we're living in the past because society
still feels my people should be treated
as less than human.

Being labeled uneducated because
We feel we haven't been taught that
to succeed you have to want more out of life.

But, every day we're faced with adversities and strife.
Feeling pressured to do what's wrong,
because we don't see what's right.

I just want to be free!

Give me strength to live,
sick of these paranoid
conspiracies that someone wants
to see our race become extinct.
The world is so chaotic
I can hardly think, so afraid I can barely blink.
My emotions are low,
I can feel my heart sink in the pit of my soul.

I'm hoping god releases this hold the devil has on me,
praying life just lets me be.
Tomorrow is a day I would love to see,
but all I truly want and really need is to be free.

The Goddess is free!

Free, no longer feeling shackled or
irrelevant to those around me.
I was once lost, but I found myself,
and then she who is me elevated to
a level that made her fearless.

A rebel with a cause, no longer placed
on pause or held back by her existence
that she would question and
ask the universe, "why am I here?"

She learned how to love again and
trust those who served a purpose in her life.
She stopped being a victim and
started living not once, but twice.

She put on her favorite jeans and
a shirt that boosted her self-esteem
and the fact that it said "Queen",
made her feel appreciated and worthy.
Those negative words used to hurt,
but now she uses them as motivation.

She tackled her doubts and gave a shout-out
to god and her ancestors for giving
her hope. Held her head high,
went from being average to being dope.

As she wrote the words to
the next chapter of her life,
she realized from here on
out she was done sacrificing
her well-being to make others
feel comfortable around her.

The moment she freed herself
is when she truly found god
and he knew then
he had found her again
as she was never lost.

Check Yourself!

Insecurities being projected while your energy is
protected from the toxic energy that lurks and
hates simply because they are hurt or miserable
at the lives they chose.

While you're on the road to success it can
sometimes be stressful but you must
keep the motivation to do your best.

I feel as though I'm being tested,
like what's the test?

Do I allow this energy to affect my vibe or
keep my toxic proof vest to protest this
unnecessary hate that lives off of making
others feel small.

It's become too much of a burden cause I know
deep down she's hurting, but I'm not the
reason for her pain, am I?

She is spreading her negative energy
with nothing to really gain.
She is unhappy with herself,
so what's really her aim?

I look in the mirror every day
and pray that I don't become
the person who is unfulfilled
and makes others feel that
way too.

Check yourself and your
insecurities. Connect with
your ancestors mentally, and
spiritually.

No one owes you but you.
If you don't like what you see
then it's up to you to fix
the issues within.

Love yourself, because
no one will love you
like you and that's
the truth!

Free, but am I really?

Free, but am I really?
Lost in my thoughts no longer
seeing clearly.

The colors you've hidden are showing,
revealing themselves.

Am I compensating or living in
the illusion of the delusions that I am free?

Free to think, free to feel,
am I existing or standing idly in life?
Questions with no answers, panic, or is it rage?
I need to sage all of this dismissive
energy to start the new chapter that
still has no words, nothing just a blank page.

What is the conclusion to my fate,
do I stand tall or break?

Am I chained to my fears with
constant insecurities that stem
from the opinions of my peers?
Time keeps ticking, as I lie here
tripping.

I can feel my anxiety increasing,
the anger and vexation releasing
me and freeing me the version of myself
who is afraid to escape
the false reality created in my mind.

Or have I been free the entire time?

Nothing to prove!

This life is what you make it
and how you choose
to live is how you choose,
but every day I feel I have
something to prove.

No matter what you do someone
is always lurking in the
shadows criticizing your moves
As if it's not on their level of success.

Even when you feel
you did your best they always
make you feel like you did less.

Am I a dream chaser or am I chasing dreams?
Whatever I'm doing I must excel and
never let the world or the ones
with defeatist opinions prevail.
I'm constantly fighting with
myself to find my purpose
and after I find it I ponder if
Is it worth it?

You know worth taking a risk?
Or the worth the sleepless nights?
I shouldn't be in a battle with my dreams
when I've already won the fight and
seen the sight of the future it holds.

But, what can you do when everything
is spiraling out of control and you no longer
feel in control of your destiny?
I really think the universe is testing me.

The truth is I got nothing to prove to them,
regardless of their thoughts or opinions.
is it I who will gain success and wealth
from the path I choose to take?
If I take the path alone because no one in
believed in me then that's the sacrifice I have to make.

Nothing to prove, cause I got nothing
to lose walking into my purpose
with my head held high,
smiling cause I didn't give up and
Instead, I continued to try.

At the end of the day when they ask how I did it?
I'll tell them it was your lack of faith
and disbelief that led me
to this destination and gave me
the will to complete my vision.

Because I never had anything
to prove to you in the first place!

Lift Your Voice!

Lift your voice and let your words
speak of passion
and power that echoes
through the hallways where we were
once segregated because our presence was
intimidating.

Let us not be limited by our fears or
be doubtful after being mocked
by our enemies or our peers.
We are kings and queens of this
generation, so let's stop fighting one another
and together we can
build a nation that will allow us
to break generational curses
and build generations of wealth.

Yes, we want to be equal but being
equal starts with self.
Self-esteem, self-love, self-value,
and self-worth, how
can we expect to be better if
we don't put ourselves first?

Lift your voice to break stereotypes
and to change societies expectations,
don't allow yourself to be
limited to potential when you
have what it takes.

Lift your voice to sing and show love
to every black king and queen who
were victims of racial violence.

Stop being afraid of the oppressor
who intimidates you to stay silent,
sing of our ancestors past, and remember
it is us and only us who can create
the revolution
while embarking on this path
of enlightenment.

So hold your head up kings and
queens cause we got this,
lift your voice and
change the status quo!

New Beginnings!

Yesterday is gone, here I stand empowered
and strong.

Today something came over me,
when I woke up, it made me
see that life is worth living when
you don't give up.

Sometimes those people who claim
they had enough are really saying
give them reasons not to give up.
Be there and help them to see
there is someone out
there they can trust.

I looked at the new faces looking back at me,
some I remember others were never in my
memory.

But, it all became clear to me that even
if you never knew or shared a moment,
this is where you start new and
own it.

No one can live your life, as well as you can,
and no one is going to plan your journey
or always hold your hand. You
have to be the overseer of your
newfound blessings, it is up
to you to live life to the fullest,
so stop stressing!

Someone out there is living their last days
and here you are crying because
things didn't go your way.
Well, this is where you wipe your tears
and face your fears.

Fix your crown, smile don't frown,
and remember who you are.
No one can dim your light,
because you're not damaged
goods, you're a star.

Life is going to take you through
twists and turns,
it's up to you which lessons or
outcomes it brings.

So cheer up, because a
new beginning is on its way,
and it's clear that today is
going to be a better day!

Walking Into Your Greatness!

Dreaming and scheming of
my future goals, nervous
but anxious to see what my future holds.

I become obsessed with success
because I know I am
destined to be great.

I just hope I haven't missed my destination
and end up getting there late.

All I want to do is
level up with no hate,
never have to cross paths
with fake congrats,
"girl you did that", with
fake smiles and laughs.

Walking into my greatness with
patience and my head held high,
no longer afraid of the
inevitable because I am a
queen, no scratch that
a goddess who's fly,
intelligent, and humble
beyond measures.

I feel no need to brag
or speak ill of others who like me
are working towards their growth
and getting better in life.

The competitive mentality is cool
but what's even greater
is when we all win and can eat together.

Let's look at one another and see our value,
go back to our community and pour into it
what was given to us,
make money while making
a difference because Black
excellence is beautiful
but Black unity is a must.

The powers we hold when we
walk into our greatness
with no pettiness,
jealousy or hatred is a power that will
revive the community
and give us keys to break
generational curses and
create generational wealth.

But, it starts with knowledge of self,
self-awareness.

Are you ready for this blessing
we are about to receive?
Can you see us doing great things?

Yes, I am a queen and you are a king,
and together
we can do anything when we
acknowledge our true
selves and walk into our greatness
with each other!

Love Poetry

Romantic Vibes I

Strangers in passing,
while our true identities yearn
for unmasking.

I see you, I feel you and
I need you in ways I never felt.

Silently, I sit alone thinking
about the cards, my life has been dealt.

Thinking if you touch me will I
reject you or melt into your hands like butter?

Secretly, I long for us to touch each other,
sweet kisses and caresses that
will leave me wanting more.
My thoughts of you playing like a movie
wondering what else is in store?
This lingering feeling is making me ruminate,
if you had my body in front of you,
how would you explore it?

Looking into your eyes is a sentiment
that's euphoric.

I can't disregard this lustful obsession
I have,
Are you a blessing or someone
that's a part of my past?

Will I have moments of laughter or tears?
I'm looking to have forever with years
of loving you like it's our last day.
No longer worried about the people around us
and what they have to say.

My heart beats for you and
that's a song I'll always play when you
enter the room and
lie next to me as we continue
on this path of love and ecstasy.

Vibing Part One

It's a 90's kind of vibe, we lay listening as
our minds get stimulated by conversations.
I intrigue you with my knowledge and empower
you with my words.

It's a late-night flow, where the vibes take us is
where we'll go. Boyz. II Men, "Please don't go",
plays next in rotation and the temptations begins,
do we sin or continue expanding our minds learning
of our ancestors past or explore one another
to pass the time?

I hit repeat on Aaliyah's "One in a million",
and express to you how you stay on my mind
and how you got me feeling. A forehead kiss
is planted upon me as I smile with joy and
playfully giggle saying "you are something
else", but it's that kind of something I want
to keep all to myself.

Vibing, as the last flame of fire flickers
on the vanilla-scented candle and the wind
outside is crying out for attention, as the
trees sway to the flow of the wind and
Aaliyah's "One in a million", comes to an
end, as we lie here vibing.

Vibing Part Two

Let me emphasize and apologize for
admiring you, but your beauty is rare.

I love the moments when we hold each
other and stare at the amazement of one another.
Let's lay in love and discover what's under these covers.

I want to be your angel and let my wings take flight,
don't be nervous because I'm taking care of you tonight.

Follow me on this rage of poetry as my word
play stimulates your body and entices your mind
with alluring thoughts.

Make room for me to lead as you breathe deeply in awe
of how my love has you longing for more.

Let's place our hands together and let our kisses
connect us and take us to another level,
we'll start slow and steady as I whisper
"my king are you ready?"

You've been loved but not like this, I got more
to offer if we choose not to let this love falter.

I'm fascinated maybe even hypnotized by the
the sight of you, in my mind, are scenarios of things I'd like to do.

But first, let me gaze upon you as if you were a
painting on the wall. Watching you from
every angle curious about the mysteries
you hold inside.

Captivate me, as I get caught
up in the rapture of you.

Fate

I can feel my senses have been heightened,
my mind awaken and enlightened by the
possibility of what could be.

It is the sweet surrender of my constant
rejection of this love that you're trying to share
with me.

Everything feels so heavenly and sounds so
peaceful, but am I your enemy or your equal?

Does love cuddle me like a child clinging to its
blanket when they are scared or a woman
clinging to her insecurities?

Will I walk into a room filled with darkness or bliss?

Reassurance comes from your words, but what if
it's sealed with a kiss.

Are you my addiction or home?
Do I stay or roam until I'm lost and
hope that you find me.

Do I lay in silence or make a sound to
express the unrest in my spirit. Is the end
near or are we finally revealing our fate that
led us to this place and forced us to awaken
from our deep denial.

As I smile, I think of the faith I'll have or
the laughs that will be ruined by tears.

Am I living to exist or existing just to
live? What gives, will we have months
or years?

Only time can be told when our
fate is exposed.

Time Stood Still

I held you in my arms and cried because
every day you tried to reach me and
teach me that life is too short and
holding grudges are wrong.

No matter how much I wanted to be angry
I chose to be strong. Instead, in my head
I was doing the right thing. But, now
I'm barely sane and in pain of losing you.

Time stood still as you wiped my tears
and I reflected on the years I wasted,
the memories that
could've been created but how when one
is filled with feelings of regret.

I can still hear your laugh and the way
you'd do anything to make me smile.
Time stood still as I shouted don't go!

Stay, for just a little while let's make
up for the memories we missed,
I'm sorry I let my anger
keep me from you.

Time stood still as I laid on your casket
and cried uncontrollably with
people I haven't spoken to in
years holding me and telling me
it'll be okay but when? Or how
when I'm burying you today,
my heart aches and my mind
is all over the place.

I'm trying, I'm really trying but
the hurt won't go away.
I have to look in the mirror
every day and think of how I
let you walk away and never
held out my hand for you to
turn around and reach.

Just writing this is making me
weak as the tears continue falling down
my cheeks I wish time stood still
so I can tell you one more time
"I love you and will see you soon."

This poem is dedicated to anyone who
lost someone, "Tomorrow is never promised",
tell your loved ones you love them everyday.

Spoken Word Half Crazy

Poetic, is what I would call us,
but the question is was it love
or us lusting over a fantasy of what
We thought love should be?

There were times when I felt
misunderstood you were the only
one who understood me.

Yet, it wasn't enough,
we let our emotions get out of control
and it manifested into toxic energy.
The way we used to be so close is
sending me and making me break down.

I feel like I'm having a breakdown
mentally of how I loved you so deep,
laid at night watched you sleep
what we had was mysterious and
now the mystery is gone it's killing me.
Tears filling my eyes from all
the lies I believed, I was so naive.

But, you promised you'd never leave
just for me to wake up one day and
find you deceived me now I'm
going half crazy.

Pretty Brown Eyes

His eyes are the window to his soul,
the way they looked deep
into mine as we lie looking up
at the night sky that exhibited

the most beautiful scenery it
was as if time stood motionless
and I could hear my heart beating
and becoming in sync
with his.

Something about you makes me feel
emancipated from my fears,
I sigh with relief at the way you wipe
my tears away.

It was like all my years of torment
and suffering had left my
mind. For a moment, we let time get
away each touch healed
apart of me, I didn't know was broken
and hereafter I remain hoping that
the memories have finally perished
and tomorrow will be a better day.

No longer do I feel tethered by my thoughts
of being alone because you came and
made my heart your home and held
my hand to show reassurance
that I've never had to feel
alone again.

Those brown eyes had a way of making
me say things and feel things I never felt.
I was more carefree and happy, able
to laugh and love without the uneasiness
of thinking loving someone was wrong.

I love that beyond those brown eyes is a man
who is caring, passionate, and strong.
His eyes mirror exactly who he is, a rarity
only so many are lucky enough to have a heart
and mind like his.

So obstinate yet understanding,
respectful and not demanding.
I love that you took the time to learn
what it takes to love someone
as fragile as me which allowed me the
time to love me in return.

I pray that we both continue growing,
learning, and loving
as I am happy to possibly forever
stare into those brown
eyes that light the window to my
soul each time they gaze into
mine.

Love Goes

Lights down low with a soft music flow,
Janet Jackson singing "That's The way love goes",
an awkward silence with intricate stares
shared between them with just limited space.
He placed his hands on her thigh as
she slowly caressed his face.
He whispered "you're beautiful",
as she smiled so shyly, then she asked
"why me?"

He smiled with a devilish grin and said
"why not", you've always been
my best friend and I loved you forever.

The universe brought us close,
but I knew we were meant to be together.
You're mine and I'm yours,
let's take our time and love
with a passion so intense that our
souls intertwine and become one
as we let love flow and that my king
is the way true love goes.

Captivated

Am I dreaming or having visions of you,
every day I become more in like,
I find myself feeling melancholy
at the thought of you not being in my life.

I know sometimes I fight my feelings
and guard my heart out of fear of getting
hurt but you taught me to see
myself more while acknowledging my worth.

How is it a person can have such
a remarkable impact and be the peace
that stops me from overthinking and
teaches me not to react to everything?

You give pleasure with your touch and
kisses that cure my pain.

I lie reflecting over your smile
and all the memories we created.

I have to admit I love it when you come
but hate when you go.

It is the excitement of seeing you again
that keeps me hold.

Your heart and warmth I desire to interlace with.

It's you, yes you who I choose to continue
investing my time with.

Take my hand and let me lead you to a place
that only appears in our dreams,
I'll enrapture you with
my words as they make love to
your mind and captivate
your soul.

I aspire to take you to the highest level
while loving you so genuinely.

Let's speak into existence this love
and fervor we seek as I captivate you
and leave you so in awe it has
you weak in the knees.

Say you're afraid, let me relieve you of any
doubt while staring into your brown eyes.

Then later I'll let you captivate me
and we'll lay after cuddling each other
as if it's the last time we'll meet.

Let me captivate you and give
you the love we both need.

I found

I found quiet, one who is rare
yet so unique.

He is divine and spiritual,
a mind so profound
and a smile that illuminates
even the most dimmed
yet gloomiest room.

The scent of your cologne makes my
heartbeat in a euphonious tone,
as I blush at your touch and
crave you when I'm alone.

Is it the glow of your melanin
or your laugh that sends cupid's
arrows shooting rays of love into
my soul making me beam with joy.

I found someone who is chivalrous
and gives me everything
even when I don't ask for a thing.

I found someone who I'll always tell
"I love you", and am grateful that you
took the time to love me and find your
way back no matter how far apart
we are in the world.

Soulmate

"We are two souls split into one."

I crave you even when you're close to me,
when I close my eyes it's your face I see.

Your brown eyes and mesmeric smile are
still etched in my brain.

I feel as if without you I would go insane.
something about your presence makes me whole.

Most would say I'm wasting my time,
but it's you who has my heart and soul.

The day we met I exhaled because
I know it's the peace that I found,
I told myself I wouldn't fall but the
the heart wants what it wants.

How do we love? Let's count the ways,
most envy what we have because it's not
a phase or an adolescent crush that never
got revealed.

What we have is everlasting and real,
you are my soulmate and best friend,
I'll admit we're not perfect and have
our days but no matter what I'm here
to stay.

So many take for granted the ones
they love and never right their wrongs,
but you and me, we're strong. We fight
for what we love because we know
where we belong.

In your arms, I feel at home and protected,
our souls are split into one and forever
connected.

Could I see me without you?
Never, because with you I want forever.
You are my soulmate, my missing piece.

A love letter to poetry

Your words have been my therapy,
my eyes opened to your clarity and
healed my soul.

You helped me get through
the darkest days, allowed me to
vent when I felt enraged. You've
been here through every stage
of my life.

Here we are in chapter 34 and like my day
one you're still here with me.
Through my heartbreaks, and mistakes
you gave me a voice to speak my peace.

I feel as though I'm your baby
that you watched grow.

Some days when I feel blocked
and my inspiration
is temporarily on hold you reach
out your pen and give me the
motivation to go on.

Playing the music to lift my spirit,
smiling along with me when that
inspiration returns and cheers me on.

You gave me the strength to go on and
stay strong.

One day I remembered
feeling alone, crying cause
I could no longer pretend to be okay,
whispered "you're not alone,
I've always been here." now
tell me what's wrong.

Say what you mean and mean
what you say, this love affair
could never end because you
became my friend guided me
when I couldn't navigate my
way out of the dark.

This letter is my praise to you,
as I'll always have a special place
for you in my heart.

If we ever part, the
memories of you will
keep me whole because
you have a piece of me
that could never be stolen
by another. You're my
healer and I'm glad
we found each other.

The Black Queen!

"Real queens fix one another's crown"

The stereotype of A Sista!

Loud and ghetto to a T, this is
the perception they have of me.
Bad attitude and eyes that could roll
all the way to the back of your head.

She may not be classy but she definitely
might be good in bed. Don't wife her,
one night her and leave the money
on the night-stand.

Go ghost, no follow back
or answer that lets her
know where y'all stand.

Sista, sista you've been warned
of the things, they say about you.
Nevertheless, despite their
grotesque, I got you.

I see a queen with big dreams
and a mind filled with ideas
that will change the world.

While society keeps labeling you
just another ghetto girl.
The brainwashing from the oppressor and
the media stops today, cause us sista's
got something to say.

You may look at me with unamused eyesand
even turn your nose up, but this sista is going to rise.
Does my melanin offend you? Why are you so upset?
Cause I walk like a queen and talk like a goddess
that lives life with no regret.

Do you feel your labels will decrease
my self-esteem? Does it make you sleep
better when you diminish and belittle my dreams?

A sista with an attitude of passion her loud mouth
speaks words of knowledge not aggression.
She rolls her eyes at those who refuse to give her
the respect she deserves and as for her class she has
surpassed and shown that she is beyond a one night stand.
This sista deserves to be treasured and pleasured with
intimacy so deep that her soul escapes her body
while freeing her mind.

Your labels only push her to keep going as she disregards
the unkind notions that she is valueless. See this is what
happens when you love yourself because the words no
longer hurt. She is beyond your stereotypical perception
because she knows her worth and has shown she is the
real true God a.k.a mother Earth. So, before you go
down talking this queen remember who she is and
respect the goddess cause she and her king was here first.

I am not my hair!

"I love my hair because it is a reflection of my soul."

Kinky, curly, or nappy, I love my natural hair and
it makes me happy to be unapologetically me and
that makes me free.

Look at your full lips, big hips and melanin
thinking you're a queen, but according
to society with that hair, skin, and body you can't win
But, I know the truth soI continue to embrace
my natural roots and transcend.

We are constantly forced to conform to the European
standards to fit in, yet when we choose to stand out
here come the culture vultures with their hands out,
Biting off of our culture and telling us we're unapproachable
and our natural hair is not suitable for corporate America.
I really wish you simple-minded people would stop
comparing us.

My natural beauty is powerful beyond measures,
I refuse to straighten it so with your hair you can do
whatever. I love my 4c hair because it is a national
treasure, many have tried to imitate it but like my
skin tone it'll never be duplicated.

Keep your perms, and skin bleach, I don't want
to see my full lips and cultural hairstyles become
a trend in your magazines and fashion scenes.

You can keep your side-eyes and stares when you
see my fro, continue looking crazy when I rock my
"I am A Black Queen", shirt and turning up your nose.

I am beautiful, and my melanin is on fleek, don't
hate me cause I shine and my melanin is unique.
Don't look at me with disgust when I speak,
I refuse to be labeled silent or inadequate.

I decided I would break the mode and
take control of me and my 4c hair
that makes me rare and uncompromising,
I am not my hair!

A True Queen!

Escaping the madness, I am done with
the sadness and material trappings of this
world. I have succumbed to my desires
and realized that I am not an average
girl. I am a goddess, a woman with
purpose who knows what her
worth is and is blessed to breathe
the air the earth gives.

Even though, she is suffocating
she still allows me to live and gives me
the drive to get up and make a difference
in myself and who those who bring joy
to my life.

I can't, I mean I refuse to let
myself be locked up in a space where
I have no room to grow or leave when I
can't bear the burdens or feel forced to
hold the weight of others issues on her
shoulder.

She is getting stronger, maybe
a little bolder she stopped letting
others demean and control her and
took back the power they stole. Her
life was once empty, but it finally
became whole.

She looked in the mirror staring at
the reflection looking back at her
and saw she was the answer to
her problems.

Like the queen she is, she stood tall
with her head high and solved them!

My Melanin is not for sale!

She wants to walk like me, talk like
me but never takes the time to see
that Black women are unique.

We're the trendsetters, who the
culture vultures aspire to be, buying
lips and butt injections just so she can
be an off-brand version of me.

Talking like a ghetto stereotype, because
the media never shows Black women in a
positive light.

Calling themselves black
queens acting as if they're the real thing,
but fail to see the disrespect or pain that
Black women go through and
face every day.

Everybody wants to be
Black but without
the struggles or adversity.

I remember a time where they'd make fun
of our hair and features, now they're paying
big money to be us. Still in silent downcast
eyes they refuse to treat us with respect,
they walk so carefreely like they're above us,
they love our culture, but don't love us.

Tell us to get over 400 years of captivity
and that racism isn't a thing, meanwhile over
a million Black women go missing and no one
says a thing.

You wonder why I get upset, when
we're the butt of society's joke because
we get tired of being nitpicked and belittled
all at the expense of someone who lacks humility
and common sense.

She says "we're jealous because she'd look
better in our skin", but trust we are the originators,
otherwise, they wouldn't try so hard to be like us.

You may get injected, but my melanin has been
popping since birth.

Yeah, you ripped off of our
culture but the sistahs, no
us queens we did it first.

My melanin is not for sale!
So take our hair and our features
off of your shelves and understand this,
no matter what surgeries you undergo
you will never be a sista because we real
Black women know a true queen when
we see her!

Facade!

She wears the mask that hides
the eyes which distract you from
her lips of lies.

"Soulless woman",
is a phrase commonly used to describe
her, those who know the true her despise
her. She portrays this sweet soul but
has a dark soul inside her that is
filled with hatred.

Hatred of the woman she has become,
a liar, a user, a repeat offender, and accuser
of others mistreating her when it is her
who holds the gun. A true victim mentally,
she has checked out of reality
and lost her common sense.

She has become so paranoid of her
surroundings, as her entitlement
is hanging on by a thread.

Something about her is
deeply disturbed, cause she doesn't
seem right in the head.

Is it the guilt of what she had done in
her past? Or shame? One can only
imagine why someone so heartless
lacks accountability but loves to
point the blame at everyone but herself.

She has created this illusion
that only she matters in the world
like she is a ruler and
the others are the help.

Facade, she wears it so casually,
so far from reality and did I
mention how she's so
narcissistic and conniving.

Women like that love thriving
off of making those who
are happy feel miserable,
cause the truth of the matter
is that facade she wears is
a cover-up for the fact that
she regrets the life she lives.

It's because of the horrible things
she did to the ones who loved her
even when she refused to love herself.

Now she has become the old angry
woman yelling at the children playing
and laughing without a care in the world.

She used to have a soul,
but no one truly knows what happened
to the girl cause of the facade,
she puts on to hide
the insecure woman she
has become.

Bye, You!

I left for the betterment of myself
no longer held hostage by you.
Cried so loud I had to turn up the
volume to drown out my sorrows
and sigh a relief.

As I am no longer haunted and taunted by
your toxic ways. I used to lay lifeless in a
daze, now I can exhale and feel the better
days coming, and the pain I used to feel
numbing.

Reduced my access to you and rejected your
abuse, at that moment I felt myself transcend,
lost an enemy, but in me, I gained a friend.

I used to think I couldn't live without you
and my life was at an end.

Now, I'm living and every day my life begins,
took that L, and now I'm getting plenty of wins.

I remember when you treated me like
a chore as if I was on your list of things to
do, I must've been dumb because I walked
around with no clue about the real you.

It hurt, but I healed used to think I
wasn't deserving of love, but now
I have so much love to give.

I felt uninspired, but look at me live.
No longer haunted and taunted by you,
closed the door left my emotional bags
and attachment on the floor, so bye you!

Fighting with her!

Fighting, constantly fighting with her to be
a better version of who she used to be.

She questions who am I, is this life yours or mine?

Am I the enemy or is it you who has brought her to the
the point of no return.

How does she escape the madness
going on inside her head?

Is she ready to admit that she's scared?

Scared of what happens once the doors open and
she is no longer held hostage by her fears
and doubts.

Will she free herself from herself and finally see
the enemy is not me but she who refuses to acknowledge
the hurt and trauma that has controlled her for too long.

I want to hold her, console her and remind her of who
she used to be, but how can I when I am her and she is me.

Settling!

Running from my worth feeling shameful for not
putting myself first.

I feel as though I've been cursed or under your spell,
whatever this is I can tell the consequences
will be me regretting the moment we met.

I get this burning yet yearning feeling whenever you're
around that, I can't escape.

I tried to forget, even ignored you a few times
and in those times you constantly cross my
mind, so I guess I'm just settling.

I suspect I'm afraid that love for me doesn't exist, as I
sit here alone in my room staring out my window and
think about the days where you treated me like gold
and now I no longer want to be held by you. I now wish
to break free of the hold you have on me.

I am a shell of my former self because even she
the confident version of me has gone into hiding
and here I lie alone crying.

Why am I so against being alone? Is it the thought
of no one loving me as much as I should love myself?
Or am I simply suffering from neglect?

Settling, am I really settling because I don't deserve
the soulmate for which the universe is patiently waiting
to send me or am I green with envy of those around me
who has found the one?

Spoken word!

I am a Nubian queen, a lover of all things
yet so many discredit my claim.
Always stealing what we kings
and queens created.

Sad, how we are the ones who are hated because
we possess a beauty no amount of money can buy.
society made a standard that deemed
melanin an unattractive thing.

So, we lost our way and stop being leaders and
instead chose to stray from our path of greatness.
Never realizing their hidden envy over our chocolate
skin, full lips, and curves that would make even the most
saved man sin.

Who says having melanin isn't as
beautiful as looking European?

Our hair is a symbol of our strength and
our eyes speaks to the souls who are damaged
and taught to indulge in self-hate.

Ever see your Nubian sista go from looking
Nubian to looking like she lost her faith?

What is it going to take to go
back to embracing our crowns?
Will we continue being the joke
of society or take a stand right now?

Our daughters and sons are watching everything
we do, so the question is queen,
when are you going to learn to love the real you?

Queen Vibes!

Don't call me broken because
I've awaken my consciousness to what's real.

You say I'm changing but I found
a voice to tell you how I really feel.

There was a time you instilled fear in me
and moments I was too blind to see
that I was being betrayed.

For a while, I wondered why others never
pitied me and it was because they
had the common sense to leave,
when I chose to stay.

Sometimes we get destroyed and
forget we have a choice to leave
the ones who
want to see us broken
or silence us and say we
have no voice.

They tell us we're worthless and mock us
in front of our peers.

We become the object of
ridicule, which fuels the
hate that starts the debate
about why they have
an issue with our presence,
and don't want us here.

They blackballed us from society
and treated us like a menace,
they kill us with no hesitation and tell
us we brought it on ourselves.

Now, I'm a motherless,
fatherless child who
will never survive or be
able to accept the fact
that someone was taught to hate me.

I sit here frantically waiting for the
grim reaper to come and tell me if
he'll spare me or if he's coming to
collect my soul.

I'm getting tired, tired of looking
over my shoulders, and being
treated as a stereotype.

I am not your enemy,
I am your equal and yes the
revolution will be televised!

Black Queen!

Beautiful melanated goddess whose presence
intimidates others the moment she walks into a
room, from her curvaceous hips to her full lips
she is the true essence of what beauty represents.

But, ever so often she is treated with so much
disrespect and discontent. She is the giver of life,
the mother to our earth, a queen at birth and
although she is sometimes misunderstood
she proves time and time again why her
presence is needed.

She bears the burden and carries the strength
of ten men when met with challenges and knows
no matter what she refuses to give up and let
the naysayers deem her lazy and incapable of
surviving on her own.

Through it all, she keeps striving and continues to
be a driving force in her community. She puts on
her brave face to enforce love and unity because we
need our Black queens and kings together
in order to carry on the fight for justice to save
our people.

She earned her crown and on those days
when she wears a frown her soul still smiles
because she knows how blessed she truly is.
She lives for herself and loves with so much
compassion. Her touch can heal a thousand
broken hearts and her words will always
inspire action because she knows her place
in this world.

She's not just a Black queen, she's a Black wombman,
who despite the stares and hatred never allows
anyone to make her feel less than. She represents
empowerment, and wears those kinky and curly coils
with honor because the hair on her head is a crown
that was given to her by her ancestors.

Black kings know to never place anyone above her.
Hold on to her as she is amazing and the most sacred
treasure for which the heavens gave. So rare, that others
try to compare but no matter what she will always be one
in a million.

Understand, what I'm feeling when I speak of my
melanated sisters who ooze confidence that makes
even the strongest man weak.

Black kings let me hear you speak about
your appreciation for one of god's greatest
creations, for she is truly a queen that
deserves all the love and respect!

My sisters, I love you!

Mentally Freeing!

Beautiful Escape

I see myself leaving, leaving all the
things that would make me at times, feel low.

Outside, I appear to be a strong woman
but inside I'm a scared little girl.

Reaching, for my mother's hand to rescue
me from feeling alone, I long for a place
that I can call home
but sadly home is gone.

The people I once called friends have
become strangers, the protective feeling
I had with them had escaped as I
now feel as though I am in danger.

My emotions erupt and I explode from
all the disappointment I've been through.
Now I stand here waiting to see my fate.

As my fate exposes itself,
I see I'm standing on the edge,
it feels as if I am about to fall
but then a hand reaches down
and as the hand reaching down,
I see it is me and know
I am the only one who can save me.

Sometimes I Cry

"Crying is cleansing for the soul."

Sometimes I sit and cry, I cry because I feel alone
or is that I've lost the will to go on.

I've given it all I got
and to be honest I don't have a lot.

Every day is a struggle, but somehow I survived.
Is it crazy that I regret that I'm alive?
I strive for my best but even my best isn't good enough.

Now I lay me down to sleep and hope this pain
will finally cease and God will show me the way
to heal, so that tomorrow will be a better day for me
to feel that I do have a reason to live.

I Am Me!

Escaping the pressures of the world's
expectation, while setting limitations
on the opinions that
everyone has of me.

Breaking free of their disapproving stares
and walking through confidently
without care.

Some say I'm different because I don't
get excited about socializing
or partying.

I tell them a good book and music is my
definition of a good time when it keeps
me sane and clears my mind.

Often, I wonder how the world
became materialistic
equating value to frivolous things
yet not appreciating
the company of those who matter.

All the while
they're faking smiles and
being subjected to
meaningless chatter.

I, however, love being in the company
of quietness and ever so often
I adore a little noise.

Yes, I do yearn for those noises that are
peaceful like the sounds of the
oceans waves or trees swaying
side to side on a windy day.

A tree branch tapping at my window
as if it was hoping
to get an invite into the warmth.

I never thought that choosing to be me
meant that I haven't experienced life,
but now here I am second-guessing
and thinking about how they
cannot see the value of themselves.

Finally Free!

Free, finally free of the neglect you gave.

Buried, I buried your existence and put it in
my mental grave blocking all the memories
of you out.

Scream, I scream in frustration but I know
yes I know I can truly say the anger I feel is out.

Cry, yes I cried but today I laughed for the first
time and it felt good to no longer dwell on
something that wasn't meant to be, wasn't
meant for me.

Relieved, I am relieved that your true self you
revealed now I can refocus my energy and restore
my faith in me.

Painting, I'm painting a mental picture of myself
being happy and no longer plagued by the
moments we spent.

Ready, I'm ready to live in tranquility to walk
barefoot on the beach and feel the wind run its
fingers through my hair while playfully touching
my cheek.

Healing, I am healing and repairing myself so that I can
get back to me that I used to be.

Fearless, I am fearless because I hold the power that
will help me to be the woman I am destined to be.

Happy, I am happy that I'm finally free and
I am ready to be courageously and
unapologetically me!

Matters of the heart!

My mind and heart are conflicted while my
actions are portraying my words.

I keep telling myself not to become a statistic
or be a victim of my own bad choices.
But, sometimes the good conscience
gets stifled by the bad voices that echo,
"do it, you know you want to."

I'm reasoning with myself to do what's
right and not be lured into what's wrong.

It's crazy how I ceased to find my
inner peace because I've yet to
let go of the indignation and
frustration that holds me hostage
each time I gain the courage to walk away.

Healing takes time, time that comes with
consumed thoughts and a broken heart
that will temporarily be damaged until
the heart and mind are no longer
battling one another.

The spirit and soul have to separate
themselves from the manipulation of
being told that they need this person
in order to feel alive.

One must be okay with being alone
and never let the thought of that person
that cost them to lose themselves again.

But what does one do when the heart, mind
and body still can feel the pain?

Faded

Faded, yes I'm faded off of the love you gave me,
feels like you're god and you're the only one
who can save me?

Crazy, cause all I do is think of you lately.
Some would say you have a savior complex
but I digress.

I use to love the way you'd comfort me with your
positive energy and then those times
you'd give me intimacy.

You could turn me on without touching me,
the way you would look at me had me lusting,
I found myself anxious to be in your embrace
while your lips I so desperately
wanted to taste.

Your face is all I see when I fall asleep,
I can still smell your cologne you know
the one that made me weak.
It gave me goosebumps when you'd caress my face
and kiss my cheek.

Now I'm having withdrawals
cause we barely speak.

I'm going through the cliche emotions where
I can't eat or sleep. I'm reminiscing about lying
on your chest and listening to your heartbeat
It was truly my favorite tune.

Meanwhile, my thoughts are preoccupied and
filled with moments we shared in my room.

Playful kisses, longing stares, jokes and
compliments, what we had was rare.

Yeah, you were my twin flame. I can admit
that it hurts to say your name. I feel as though
We were both to blame.

Did we only seek to cause each other pain or
love one another, I mean what was really the gain?

Is it all a game or am I standing here with a hint
of shame while waiting at your door hoping you'll
open it and we'll explore where we went wrong or
should I just go home?

Damn, the radio is playing our song. I'm trying but
I can't go on until I know if what we had is worth
fighting for.

My Destination

I'm tired of settling for good enough and being lowered to potential.

I want more in life besides struggle and strife, but that struggle makes me humble.

Sometimes I find myself about to stumble and fall, but my pride won't let me.

I stand tall, ready and willing to fight this battle, I know most rather admit defeat, but that's not my cup of tea.

I keep telling myself every day your destination is going to lead you to your blessing.

I smile even when I want to frown because I refuse to keep stressing.

Trapped

I've become a prisoner in my mind,
trapped with no escape while contemplating
the times and days I've been held captive.

I try to find light, but my vision is still hazy and
yet to be clear.

I wonder as I sit in the dark if I have a reason
to be here.

I feel the walls closing in, I wonder if this is the
end if someone will rescue me from this
cruel fate, or am I destined to be left in this
dark place.

I've become a prisoner in my mind,
trapped pondering my escape,
I lie still hoping the sunlight will
reveal itself, and save me from me,
but there is no way out.

I scream, I shout, let me out!
Please let me out!

I just want to get out of this prison
and free from this eerie place,
I call my mind.

Message to the old me!

Many nights of silent cries, and constant
fears. Yet all I can feel are the tears running
down my face, with no one there to embrace.

Memories of disappointment need to be
erased.

Wishing I had someone to replace and
fill the void of emptiness in my heart.

It's funny how you can go from talking to
everyday to barely speaking and now even
though you're in the same place I feel we're
miles apart.

I call out your name but no answer, it's
becoming so sickening that it makes me weak.

I can recall a time we were close and now you've
disappeared and went ghost.

I look up at the stars to see if you're there, but
your soul is still here.

I shed another tear wishing I could feel you
but nothing compares to the real you.

I lay here in agony, no clue as to where you
went. I imagine being near you, maybe it's
because to me you were heaven-sent.

Missing person sign going up. if you
this woman let her know she is loved
and I miss her. I hope I find her soon.

Message to the old me!

Escaping My mental prison

Elevation, is what I'm trying to do
but my self-doubt won't let me
make it through the doors which leads to
my blessings.

I keep trying to think positive only to
end up stressing and protesting that
my dreams aren't meant to come
true and maybe this life is all I have to
look forward too.

Manifestation is my aim, but I keep getting into
my own way and causing myself pain
because I refuse to see my
way out of this mental prison that
holds hostage my dreams.

The escape plan is in full effect,
still, I haven't found the confidence
to leave and once again I find myself trapped
inside my head.

Depression, I fought but anxiety plotted
and schemed then won leaving me
feeling like I'm on the run from
myself and every time
I think I'm free, the chains
of doubt grab a hold of me.

So what do I do? I yearn for freedom
but am scared to embrace it,
I have the doorway that leads
to opportunity but don't have
the courage to open it and take it.

I am the key to my success,
but how can I unlock
the door if I haven't
unlocked my potential
to free me from myself?

Black Kings

The Black King

"We must value our men!"

A warrior in his right, some would deem him a knight.
But, to me he is a King, a Black King.
Although sometimes he is misunderstood
he does what can and still remains a good man.

Society often has its foot on his neck,
constantly targeting him with
so much disrespect and disregard,
but like the king he is,
He plays his part.

Often imitated but never duplicated because
he the original African god.
Strong, loving, and beautiful with a
deep-spirited mind.

Powerful beyond measures and might I add
he takes pride in loving his queen
while showering her with
knowledge and pure pleasure.

His words still echo in my mind,
"you are my queen and
together we can get through anything."

He feels my pain and soothes it with his touch,
his kiss is like
magic, when our lips lock my heart stops
and my body tingles with
senses I never even knew I had.
Some would call him a statistic and
say it's unrealistic that a man like him exist,
but sisters let me tell you this, I prayed for this man.

I even made a list of everything I desired,
and to me, he was sent. I admire his strength,
confidence, and sacrifices he makes to protect his own,
how he is so driven and takes care of his home.

A man that is god-fearing and not afraid
to show his emotions, he isn't afraid to love
because that is one of his many gifts that he
was sent to give.

I love this man, for he is the reason
I truly adore and value our
Black men.

So many try to count him out, but never
will I leave him to feel as if he has to face
this world alone. Because as long as he has
his queen as he told me before, we can get
through anything!

Respect to our Black men!

My Crush

His smile illuminates every room and fills it with
happiness that only he can bring.
His laughter is the cure to my pain,
when he speaks my name I blush
because for the first time in years
I never thought I see the day I'd have a crush.

I love his deep mind and beautiful soul,
something about a man that when
he talks you stop and listen because not
only are his words powerful but his intelligence is intriguing.

My heart skips a beat when he enters the room and somehow
that chaotic place that once felt dark is now lit up with an
aura so intoxicating that for a moment it feels as though
he and I are the only ones standing there staring into
each other's eyes.

But, even then it is a thought that constantly lingers in my mind.
Will I ever have a chance to reveal my true feelings or be faced
with the realization that I have the shyness of a 16 year old,
after being kissed for the first time.

My God Sent King

Feels as though my breath is being ripped from
my chest and I'm slowly but surely losing control.

As the walls start to close in,
I hear your voice and see your hand
reach out to save me telling me to
take deep breaths and that everything
will be alright.

Yet, when you're not here I can't sleep at night,
I long for your arms to be wrapped me because
when they are I feel protected.

The world isn't against me when you're near and
any negative thoughts I get I reject.

Something about your presence that
makes me feel at peace.

When you stare I smile at the fact you took
the time to be patient and love me as I
have loved you.

Now I wonder what is next and how I was
so deserving of a king who truly values his
queen, I mean the way your words and
touch eases my pain or how I giggle at
the way you say my name.

I can't say what will happen tomorrow
or even in a year, but I will admit that I
love having you here with me and
there's no other place I'd rather be
then here with my god-sent king.

His Halo

He is and will always be an angel sent to
protect his queen, some say he's useless but
I digress because he is everything.

Everything a woman needs, he exceeds every
expectations no matter what problem or trial
he faces.

I see your halo, love how your skin glows and
arms wrap around me so gently and I'm so
ecstatic that you found me.

I can't say enough of how lucky we are to have
you Black man so I wrote this poem to make you
understand that your presence is valued despite
anyone's opinion you are appreciated.

So hush and stop speaking ill of yourself cause
your Black queens love you when no one else
sees how having you is the best gift the universe
could give.

I love you and with you, I no longer live in fear of
being taunted because you stand by my side even
when the enemy wants us to divide and
fight against each other.

I just want to say Black king, my brother you
are worthy even though society says otherwise.
Wear that halo proud and keep being the warrior,
the king that the ancestors gave to us beautiful
melanated queens!

Weaponising Our Blackness!

"What do you want to be when you grow up?"

Alive, is what I tell myself but what you can do
when your life is only valued by you and the same one's
killing you do with it no remorse or no thought
of your family in mind.

They weaponize your blackness and see it as a weapon,
and get mad when it's your blackness that you're protesting
to protect. They lie and tell the media "I thought he or she
had a weapon", but nothing was found. So, was there a
personal reason for you to end up dead on the ground?

Screaming how you can't breathe, but they ignore your
pleads and tell you to stop resisting but the real truth is
you didn't resist they just didn't care to listen.

Weaponize, the statistics are getting higher and
the Black community is growing tired of telling
the world why Black lives matter especially when
you disregard our cries and tell us to comply.

Otherwise, we wouldn't die but really you're telling
us lies, just ask Philando Castille, but wait he complied
and you still didn't let him live. He was shot dead in front
of his family, now they're traumatized and left without him,
no punishment for the officer he gets the luxury to be alive.

Speaking of alive, let's talk about all the other brothers and
sisters whose lives came to end all because they see our
blackness as a weapon and get mad because our melanin is
a gift we were blessed with.

But, to them, it's a curse because at birth there
were targets placed on our backs and the fact
that they laugh or show no sympathy for killing
us is a reality to what they think our life is worth, nothing.

We aren't seen as human or equals,
the proof is in the racial system put in place to
oppress us more. We face injustice, discrimination
but are gaslighted to ignore all the things that
keep us held down and held back.

The truth is they hate us, yeah I said that!
Weaponize, you weaponize us because our
blackness represents greatness.

The truth is they hid our history from us because
if we found out we would rise up and walk into
our greatness.

My blackness is not a weapon,
it's a blessing and
Black lives will always matter!

Ego Tripping!

Miscommunication

Words like actions matter, but what if our
actions shattered the words we speak,
would it be a deal-breaker?

I find myself wondering sometimes what
you're thinking and if your thoughts often
reflect mine. But, even your energy at times
sends mixed signals that leave me feeling like
we're one-sided.

Am I more into you than you are into me or
have I exhausted all of my time trying to be what
I seek.

I provide love, compassion, and loyalty not asking
for a lot but a little reciprocity would be the equivalent
of spoiling me.

No, I don't need constant reassurance just something
that lets me know you care. If there is a crisis even if
it's a small gesture I'd like to know you'd be there.

The problem is we often miscommunicate what we desire
and become discouraged when we don't get what we deserve.

I've grown tired of the backhanded reactions, I'm no
longer amused by dope personalities and undeniable
chemistry or attraction, if your energy doesn't match
the vibe you give then maybe it's time to fall back and
find out how we feel.

Damage

Once fragile written on the box
that contains my heart.
Yet, I faced my fears and to you I gave it.

I let down my guard and open the gates
to let you in, how you love me
determines if this lasts or ends.

You could damage the already damaged part of me,
or be my peace.

There were times I took myself for granted
and didn't see my worth.

But, today I'm learning to put
myself first.

Are you a blessing or a lesson?
Will I be protected or end up
protesting to your attempt to love me?

Will you see my flaws and run or face this love
head-on.

Falling, feeling while healing, and
sometimes shielding but willing to
give you all of me along with the key
to my heart.

Am I worth it?
Do you want me to be perfect
or can you handle my imperfections?

Are you listening, as I sit here confessing how
afraid I am, afraid of wondering if this is going
to be where our journey ends or if it's where it begins.

Hold me, and console me, I may appear strong
but truly I can only hold back for so long.

I could be damaged or just paranoid of the past
experiences I've had. Maybe,
I'm fearful of ending up with a
man like the ones from my past.

Either way, I refuse to be misled, or am I
misleading myself by thinking you're not
the one when you've been here the whole time.

I am Ego-tripping!

He saw me, I saw him across the room then he
walked over and leaned close as could as he
whispered, "you are beautiful beyond measures."

He then began to feel my body and
saw the fire in my eyes when as he
proceeded to find my buried treasure.

He asked "could I be the one",
I laughed and said it's whatever.

See my ego tripped and slipped but I
was so good he refused to dip. Almost
melted when he kissed my lips.

Felt him as he caressed my hips.
my ego then did a double trip.

I stood there lusting as he rubbed
my soft brown skin, then I gave him
a grin and for a moment I sinned.

He continued his search until
it came to an end.
My ego smiled and laid there
feeling satisfied, I felt as though I
had been reborn, purified.

He looked at me, I looked at him,
and we both smiled.

You can talk that talk, but
you would walk the walk
to, if your ego tripped you.

Cause I am ego tripping!

I Won't

I'm becoming a product of your
insecurities. He projects,
I protect and neglect the signs.

You can't make me trust if I won't and
I can't say I'm happy if I don't feel anything
but misery even at the sound of your voice.

Silence is my reaction to your constant
disrespect, I try to see the bright side but
it's so dark, dim no blue skies or white
clouds, just a shaded gray.

I cry I laugh, I pray but it never changes
the mood just temporarily makes the pain go away.

Am I a victim or an enabler of your behavior?
Do I see an out or am I more comfortable being in?

In denial, incapable of expressing
how I won't be your emotional punching bag,
your comfort when you burn bridges.

You can make me trust you if I won't and I can't
I'm happy if I don't feel anything but misery even
at the sound of your voice. I won't admit out loud
how I rejoice and feel free moments you aren't around.

I used to worship the ground you walk on,
now I have thoughts of it swallowing me whole
to escape this prison of depression.

I am standing here in hopes that
the door leads me to a place of peace and your
existence to me will no longer matter.

Your prison of toxic love I refuse to
stay in, so I'm walking away and I won't
be returning to your Discomfort Inn.

Thank you to everyone who has supported me and to my new readers, I hope you enjoy every poem, and it provides you with love, encouragement, and the power to heal.